No Child Shall Left Behind

Parenting

Dr. Johane Harrigan

ISBN 978-1-967361-10-6 (Paperback)
ISBN 978-1-967361-11-3 (Ebook)

Inquiries and Book Orders should be addressed to:

Leavitt Peak Press
17901 Pioneer Blvd Ste L #298, Artesia, California 90701
Phone #: 2092191548

Introduction

"No Child Should Left Behind" is one of the most significant concepts because every species for everyone desires to be healthy. Jesus said, "Beloved, I wish above all things that you mayest prosper and be in health, even as your soul prosper." (Isa. 53:5 NIV), "Jesus, was pierced for our transgressions, He was crushed for our iniquities; the punishment that brought us peace was on him, and by His wounds we are healed." There is nothing such as uncurable diseases because the provision has been made.

We must walk by faith to activate the blessing. Because Jesus said, "By His stripes, we are healed. We must walk in victory by God's grace to receive the healing. God desires us to heal and prosper in every area of our lives. For, nothing should be impossible for the ones who believe. There is something so significant about fasting, prayer, and faith. Through prayers, the wall of Jericho, fell, through prayer, Esther won the battle, and through prayer and fasting Jesus won the battle of temptation. The woman with the issue of blood discovers healing by faith and prayer. Healing, restoration, and prosperity are yours when you believe you are entitled to be healed. Nothing is impossible when you believe. For, God can rejuvenate everything dry in your life just as He did for Lazarus. (Joh. 11: 38-44 NIV), "Jesus, once more deeply moved, came to the tomb. It was a cave with a stone laid across the entrance. "Take away the stone, and Lazarus came out by God's commands..."

The moment we fast, pray, and reconcile to God. He grants us access to everything, on earth, in heaven, and beneath powerful. Faith plays a significant role in prayer, healing, and fasting. Apart from work faith is useless, that's why it is essential to step in for your miracle. God said you are healed. As you are healed you must do everything compatible with being healthy. Fast, pray, exercise, and eat healthily. (Joh. 5:8 NIV), "Jesus said to the blind man. "Get up! Pick up your mat and walk." So, faith allows him to act, by God's command. For everything is conceivable through faith. Be healed! Our lives matter to God for we are His people. And that was the main reason He came to die on Calvary for sins. Jesus loves and cares for us unconditionally. And that's why He wants you to experience His grace, mercies, and love. "Now to Him who can do immeasurably more than all we ask or imagine, according to his power is at work within us." My hope for you is that this book inspires you to receive healing, prosperity, and deliverance. So, that you can be a blessing for your loved one and your community and be reconciled to God for a brighter lifestyle.

"No Child Should Left Behind" Living a healthy life gives us the insights to see beyond and soar above at the highest pinnacle. Psychologically, physically, and financially. Being healed is essential in many perspectives. Being in good health enables us to experience greater miracles, joy, love, peace, and not only that but also draw closer to God's intimacy to receive every blessing God has for us. We need to heal therefore; we can establish a good relationship with God's body and be responsible for growing powerfully and spiritually. (3 Joh.2:2 NIV) "Beloved, I wish above all things that thou mayest prosper and be in health, even as thy soul prospered." "Happiness lies, first of all, in health." (George William).

Acknowledgments

I thank my children Jordan and Paul who have been such great sources of inspiration in life. They have given me a reason to wake up daily to fulfill my purpose. For every one of us, it has been created for a unique purpose. Mainly, I also want to give reverence to my Lord and Savior, the great Shepherd in my life who's strengthened and supported me, and in many ways to become an author; I never saw coming. (1 Cor.15:57 NIV), "Thanks be to God! He gives us the victory through our Lord Jesus Christ."

I dedicated this book to everyone who is sick and believes in God for a turnaround. I also dedicated this book to every destitute, every rejected one. May God Almighty shower His blessings upon us Mightily. I also dedicated this book to everyone who wants to be saved, because there is life after death. Besides, the Lord God had already paid the price for our sins. According to (John 3:16 NIV), "God so loved the world that He gave His one and only Son, that whoever believes in him shall not perish but have eternal life." How do you perceive God's love, in terms of His sacrifice on Calvary? Believers shall never forget God's sacrifice on the Cross. For the fear of God is the beginning of wisdom." for wisdom is the center of all! "Come and taste that the Lord is Good." Will you come with us?

To believe Again is essential; as the Ends time is approaching. Why we need to reconcile to Jesus? We need to reconcile to because, when we live this earth, we can live with Him in paradise for there is life after death. (Joh.11:24:25 NIV), "Martha answered, "I know he will rise again in the resurrection at the last day." Jesus said to her, "I am the resurrection and the life. The one who believes in me will live, even though they die." We need to believe again therefore, we can establish the intimacy to draw closer to Him, and growth powerfully.

For our lives to be renewed or Sharpe in different directions we need to believe and learn God's ethics and principles to get ready for His returns! (Mark.13:32 NIV). "Of that day and hour no one knows, not even the angels in heaven, nor the Son, but only the Father." Are you ready? Would you like to be ready? "The Lord is king over the whole earth. On that day there will be one Lord, and his name the only name."

Acknowledgments

I dedicated this book to everyone who was once believed in and found themselves where they once were. I also dedicated this book for everyone who would like to know more about God's plans for their lives as the Ends time is near. I also dedicated this book to everyone who wants to be saved, because there is life after death. Besides, the Lord God had already paid the price for our sins. According to (John 3:16 NIV), "God so loved the world that He gave His one and only Son, that whoever believes in him shall not perish but have eternal life." How do you perceive God's love, in terms of His sacrifice on Calvary? Believers shall never forget God's sacrifice on the Cross. For the fear of God is the biggening of wisdom." for wisdom is the center of all!

Chapter #1

EVERY CHILD IS DIFFERENT

Every child is different than another and this is the beauty of every species. Despite the differences, they all have different gifts and are "unique." Every gift is crucial in the world. E.g., We as a body as much as the legs and the arms are different no one can say they aren't a part of each other. (1 Cor. 12:20-22 NIV), "As it is, there are many parts, but one body. The eye cannot say to the hand, "I don't need you!" And the head cannot say to the feet, "I don't need you!" On the contrary, those parts of the body that seem to be weaker are indispensable. Often, the child who seems so different is the most charming child among the rest. It doesn't matter how different your child is valuable in God's eye. E.g., Rachel and are sisters. Yet they describe Rachelle as the prettiest one. Yet the father by the name of Laban still did not want Rachel merry with Jacob first. He made a strategy for Leyah to marry Essau first.

Every parent has a responsibility towards their children, and every need must be met for them to fulfill their destiny. Every child's needs are different than the other. However, every parent must know what he/her needs is/are. And strives to achieve them. Every parent has to ask themselves who I am. And that will follow their responsibility as a mother or a father. Whatever your responsibilities are, ensure that you fulfill them. How well do you know your children? What do they want to become? It should be every parent's responsibility to stand on behalf of their children's future. Some of them you cannot do much, yet we should never give up. Every season brings something different. What would you like to take place in your children's future? What support would you be willing to provide as a dad/mom? What's the dream of your children?

According to (Gen. 25:27-28 NIV), "The boys grew up, and Esau became a skillful hunter, a man of the open country, while Jacob was content to stay at home among the tents. Isaac, who had a taste for wild games, loved Esau, but Rebekah loved Jacob. As parents, we should never allow differences to stop us from performing the duty we owe to every child. Every child has different needs that need to be met by their parents. How do you manage the differences in your children's lives particularly if you have tweens? The difference is so profound that's what brings forth genuineness in them. Often it is best for every one of them. Let us find a reason to love, support, and celebrate each child despite their conditions and differences! So, they can obtain a brighter future. God's desire is for them to be fruitful and multiply. "Beloved, I wish above all things that you mayest prosper and be in health, even as thy soul prospered." Every parent wants their children to be prospered.

"E.g. "God's **promise**: **Esau**'s descendants grew into a powerful nation, affirming that God**'s** plans are intricate, far-reaching, and endure across generations." Esau was a hunter, and Jacob was quiet often by his mom. Esau's hair was red, hue, and covered in hair. Jacob fools Esau for his birthright. After the betrayal, they break up and are separated into different places. After a long time, they reconciled. (Gen. 33: 4), "Esau ran to meet Jacob and embraced him; he threw his arms around his neck and kissed him. And they wept." As parents, we should always remember the power of love and forgiveness.

Perhaps your children are in captivity or an orphanage. What do you promise your child? I want you to know that your presence plays a significant role in your children's spiritual lives. Jacob's mom ensured that Jacob obtained the blessing. "Man proposes yet God disposes Jacob encountered lots of problems in his life. "No Child Should Left Behind." Don't give up on your children!

How do you "value" your children? Children have been defined as genuine and a gift from above. Value plays a magnificent role in every child's life. The body of Christ is considered as the lilies, the apples. And the offspring in God's eye. The way you value your child will inspire you to invest in their future so that the future will be bright. Most people enjoy fruits. However, the fruit does not just happen to be in the tree. It requires a process, and the process demands to be maintained daily with the proper nutrients to nurture and bring forth good crops. You may not appreciate your children because they do not like other children you know. But it is not too late to bring forth whatever they might lose in their past. What is your duty to your child/children? What are your promises to them? Promise is one of the most important elements that always inspires people to do the impossible. It comes with will, responsibility, and commitment. "Train your children off on the way they should go, and even when they are old, they will not turn from it." Teach them to be dependable, reliable, confident, and positive. As much as Jacob and Essau's gift was different. Yet that did not define them as becoming what God intended for them to be. "Every child is matter and none of them shall left behind.

Chapter #2

"No Child Should Left Behind"

Every parent has a duty to their loved ones. Don't let go of your child for any simple reason. And Don't Give up on Your Children whatever that reason may seem to be, for you are the cornerstone of your child. Sometimes unreasonably we do things toward ourselves and our loved ones that we are not proud of. Make a wise choice for your loved ones. Parents represent a force or a tower to love, protect, and guide their loved ones in any given situation and no one can play our duty than us. Parents can bring comfort healing and restoration in times of despair. Parents represent the neon in the darkness for their families.

As parents, we represent the Book of Life for our loved ones. That is why it is essential we play fair and what we do and say in front of our children. Whatever you want our children to become in their future we must begin to plan the seed today and they will emulate it. Children have been defined as genuine and a gift from above. Value plays a magnificent role in every child's life. The body of Christ is considered as the lilies, the apples. And the offspring in God's eye. The way you value your child will inspire you to invest in their future so that the future will be bright. Most people enjoy fruits. However, the fruit does not just happen to be in the tree. It requires a process, and the process demands to be maintained daily with the proper nutrients to nurture and bring forth good crops. You may not appreciate your children because they do not like other children you know. But it is not too late to bring forth whatever they might lose in their past. What is your duty to your child/children? What are your promises to them? Promise is one of the most important elements that always inspires people to do the impossible. It comes with will, responsibility, and commitment.

Every parent has a responsibility towards their children, and every need must be met for them to fulfill theirs. Every child's needs are different than the other. However, every parent must know what he/she needs is/are. And strives to achieve them. Every parent has to ask themselves who I am. And that will follow their responsibility as a mother or a father. Whatever your responsibilities are, ensure that you fulfill them. How well do you know your children? What do they want to become? It should be every parent's responsibility to stand on behalf of their children's future. Some of them you cannot do much, yet we should never give up.

Every season brings something different. Your children might have been so abused today yet who knows what tomorrow holds. Perhaps tomorrow will be sunshine. So, keep hope in the center of your heart. Don't give up on your children keep their dreams close to your heart for God is faithful and He never fails. The wish you have for them is not impossible. If you believe and find a reason to love, protect and support them. Soon everything dream will be okay it is just a matter of time. Hold on firm. (Matt.11:28-30 NIV), "Come to me, all you who are weary and burdened, and I will give you rest. Take my yoke upon you and learn from me, for I am gentle and humble in heart, and you will find rest for your souls. For my yoke is easy and my burden is light."

Parents can be physically impaired or damaged. Yet we can never let go of our responsibility toward our children. That is the Lord God encourages us to bring the burdens to His feet for He cares. How many times have we been hurt by our children? What can we do? But to forgive and let go and let God be God. Most teens tend to disrespect their parents when they face that moment, they think that they are already mature enough even to move on by themselves.

As they don't need our support any longer. We pray that the decision that they make is the wise one. But if it is not what we should do is try to perceive them at their level of understanding and reconcile with them. And if we refuse to defuse the fire it might be hard on themselves as well as the parents too.

The Story of the Lost Sheep. It says in (Matt. 18:12-14 NIV), "What do you think? If a man owns a hundred sheep, and one of them wanders away, will he not leave the ninety-nine on the hills and go to look for the one that wandered off? And if he finds it, truly I tell you, he is happier about that one sheep than about the ninety-nine that did not wander off. In the same way, your Father in heaven is not willing that any of these little ones should perish." And that was the reason the father of the prodigal son did. It is said in (Luke. 15:11-12 NIV), "Jesus continued: "There was a man who had two sons. The younger one said to his father, 'Father, give me my share of the estate.' So, he divided his property between them." So, the younger son asks his father for his portion of the family estate as an early inheritance. As soon as he receives the potion he takes off on a long journey to a distant land and begins to waste his fortune on wild living lavishly. When the money runs off a strange famine hits the country and the son finds himself in dire issue. He takes a job feeding pigs. Overall, he becomes desperate, so destitute that he wishes to eat the same food as the pigs. Then suddenly he came to himself and returned to his father's home. And the father was so glad to receive him back. And the older brother got so jealous of the fact, the father made him a feist and the father said to him, "Your brother was lost, and he returned home that is why I congratulate him." But you have been with me and everything I have is still yours. It doesn't matter how hard the pain has been. Yet reconciliation is worth it all. How do you view forgiveness and reconciliation as parents? "No child shall leave behind." Don't let go of your children because of their behavior. The circumstances will change. "There can be no keener revelation of a society's soul than the way in which it treats its children." (Nelson Mandela).

Chapter #3

THE FUTURE IS BRIGHT

Children are not simply great the way you want them to be. The seed must be planted and nourished, particularly by the parents. Life has a lot to teach us. "Embrace the unknown, for it holds the keys to your brightest future," Jesus said in (Jer.29:11 NIV), Jeremiah 29:11: "For I know the plans I have for you," declares the Lord, "plans to prosper you and not to harm you, plans to give you hope and a future." The future can be frightening, particularly in this uncertain life. Yet with a good train that you have been invested in your children's lives, they will find the courage that they need to venture into every horizon with confidence. Building a future for your loved ones can be frustrating yet the easiest way to do it is one at a time. And believe knowing that you are not alone. One day these two challenges pass. It says in (Revelation 21:4 NIV), "He will wipe every tear from their eyes. There will be no more death or mourning or crying or pain, for the old order of things has passed away." There is hope for you and your family.

Intuition is to trust in the Lord with all your heart and learn not on your understanding. May the Lord grant you the courage that you need to overcome every struggle that seems impossible in the lives of your children. Yet, "No child shall left behind." Don't give up on your children. As is well and the best being still yet to come. It not enough to say that you love your children yet the commitment to remain despite your emotions. Sometimes it is good to release our emotions, yet if our emotions will cause pain and damage to our children, it is best to keep them from within. It says in (Pro.4:23 "Above all else, guard your heart, for everything you do flows from it." Above the pain and frustration, we must find a way to manage our emotions because we don't say anything during frustration and regret. You will keep in perfect peace those whose minds are steadfast because they trust in you." "Jesus the peace that I give you is not as the world gives." So, allow your heart to be at peace.

What would you like to take place in your children's lives five years from now? Write it down and frame it; in terms of support, responsibility, and commitment. What support would you be willing to provide as a dad/mom? What's the dream of your children? Whatever the dream is you are the source of that dream. No child should suffer any type of solitude, or loneliness of their parent's love, support, protection, and kindness. Every parent has a responsibility toward their loved ones. How do you view your presence in the life of your loved ones? I sometimes praise the Lord just to be able to provide what a parent should be to their child. What you invested in your loved ones' lives today will be reciprocated onto you explicitly. What books or organizations have you been presenting to your children lately? "If you want your children to be intelligent, read them fairy tales." — Albert Einstein

A Child's Destination

Every destination requires a firm destination to know the perfect path to take. Our feet will never take us where our hearts have not been. Preparation is essential because no one wants to be on a path that he/she doesn't want to be. Whatever your destination is you must ensure that you are in the right direction. Jesus if anyone (Jam.1:5 NIV), "If any of you lacks wisdom, you should ask God, who gives generously to all without finding fault, and it will be given to you." Every parent should be a beacon of hope and a source of knowledge to their children. In this modern day, children of this age see and do things differently. However, the job of the parents is to protect, love, and guide.

As parents, the way we view happiness is different than the way they see it. As a parent, you may value things other than happiness because happiness will fade away, yet joy and reliance will never decrease. As parents, we have to bring forth dependency, confidence, strong faith, and intuition in our children's lives despite lack-ness and criticism of this world; to know their values do not come from outward but internally. Materialism is good yet there is something much more than success particularly if you have not earned it accurately. King Solomon was one of the most influential men on the planet. He regrets his wasted life. He said vanity of (Eccl. 1:2-11 NIV), "Vanity of vanities, says the Preacher, vanity of vanities! All is vanity. What does man gain by all the toil at which he toils under the sun? "You are the bows from which your children as living arrows are sent forth." (Kahlil Gibran).

Leah & Rachell:

According to (Gen. 29:18-30 NIV) Jacob was in love with Rachel and Laban's father tricks Jacob gave him Leah, the older sister to marry instead of Rachel the one Jacob loved and worked for seven years to obtain. Laban said, "It's better that I give Rachel to you than to some other man. Stay here with me." So, Jacob served seven years to get Rachel, but they seemed like they were only a few days for him because of his love for her. The father said, "It is not our custom here to give the younger daughter in marriage before the older one. Finish this daughter's bridal week; then we will give him Rachel as one. Jacob made love to Rachel also, and his love for Rachel was so much greater than his love for Leah. According to Joh.10: 10 NIV), Keep alive in your heart the Lord God knows what you want. (Jer. 1:5 NIV), "Before I formed thee in the belly I knew thee, and before your comets forth out of the womb I sanctified thee, and I ordained thee a prophet unto the nations." If your life is meant to be bright you will be, and no one will take your blessing away. Be active and let God guide your step. Allow your life to be empowered. So, that you can be vigilant for your loved ones for the enemy comes to kill and destroy. As a parent, we are mindful of knowing that our battles are abnormal. Fight for the future of your children for, "No child shall left behind." Don't give up on your children for they are the future of the next generation.

The thief comes only to steal and kill and destroy; I have come that they may have life and have it to the full. Often, we barely explain what happens to our children. For their battle is abnormal. (Eph. 6:12 NIV), "Our struggle is not against flesh and blood, but against the rulers, against the authorities, against the powers of this dark world, and the spiritual forces of evil in the heavenly realms." That is essential to know your children and stand behind them. As parents what do you want for your children? I believe Rebecca wanted Jacob to be wealthy, and happy. Yet above riches, joy, love, and peace are essential. Materials stuff will fade away, yet joy, peace, and love will remain. To enjoy life to the fullest is amazing, yet life does not consist only of money, gold, and diamonds, it all depends on what you long for. (Joh 14:27 NIV), "Peace I leave with you; my peace I give you. I do not give to you as the world gives. Do not let your heart be troubled and do not be afraid." As our battles are abnormal, we simply need to believe in God and have confidence knowing that God is able, and we can do all things through Christ Jesus who strengthens us.

Some parents don't value their children due to their poor choices or their options. However, life is better than riches. With life there is hope. Jesus said, in this life will find problems. (Joh.16:33 NIV), "I have told you these things, so that in me you may have peace. In this world, you will have trouble. But take care! I have overcome the world." As you have already overcome it you simply need to rejoice. There is no need for frustration. As parents, we need to have discernment to perceive issues to manage every negative emotion that we may encounter and know how to manage every crucial difficulty. Jesus advises us in this life we will encounter lots of problems in this world. Yet we must convince ourselves knowing that all is well. For the Lord God is with us.

Passion to Rejoice

Rejoice: What is the concept of rejoicing? "The Lord God has defined, "rejoicing as a state of joy, celebration, and in terms of gratitude for God's goodness." I like John's Calvin statement. "There is not one blade of grass, there is no color in this world that is not intended to make us rejoice." (John Calvin). (Jam.1:2-4 NIV), "Consider it pure joy, my brothers and sisters, whenever you face trials of many kinds, because you know that the testing of your faith produces perseverance. Let perseverance finish its work so that you may be mature and complete, not lacking anything.

Parents, we can be hard-pressed as the clay, yet we are strong. Apostle Paul said in (2 Cor.4:8-12 NIV), "We are hard pressed on every side, but not crushed; perplexed, but not in despair; persecuted, but not abandoned; struck down, but not destroyed. We always carry around in our body the death of Jesus, so that the life of Jesus may also be revealed in our body, for we who are alive are always being given over to death for Jesus' sake, so that his life may also be revealed in our mortal body. So then, death is at work in us, but life is at work in you. The odds may be against daily. Yet we choose to rejoice due to, "God's promises to us." It says in, (Rom. 12:12 NIV), "Be joyful in hope, patient in affliction, faithful in prayer." It says in (Matt. 11:13 NIV), "Blessed are you when they revile and persecute you, and say all kinds of evil against you falsely for My sake. Rejoice and be exceedingly glad, for great *is your* reward in heaven, for so they persecuted the prophets who were before you." Rejoice is a choice solely you can activate. For the Lord God has given us joy every morning." Nothing can take it away when you choose to be happy.

Despite the odds we can decide to be happy always for so many blessings He had brought us; if we have to be honest; in terms of life, peace, and happiness. We as believers should never forget that we are already overcome. You have the power to overcome every battle. E.g. "I will love thee, O Lord, my strength. The Lord is my Rock, and my fortress, and my deliverer; my God, my strength, in whom I will trust; my buckler, and the horn of my salvation, and my high tower."

We can be joyful knowing that God has our back in every struggle and be at peace.

To manifest joyfully should not be a problem; for "the joy of the Lord is our strength." The moment we establish our relationship we God. He established everything we need to go by. We are the ones that must activate it. Faith is a source that generates everything we can imagine; that is why God has given us a measure of faith. According to, (35: 9 NIV), "Then my soul will rejoice in the Lord and delight in His salvation." Everything has been folds and salvation; for there is life in salvation. There is life to the fullest in salvation the way people perceive us is not how the Lord God sees us. So, it is vital that we learn to be joyful. Whether our prayers have been answered or not; we can decide to be joyful for what He has done, and for everything He is about to do through prayer and thanksgiving. In these modern days, you may encounter lots of problems that can stop you from being grateful to God. Yet, you must find a reason to just do it. The Lord said I have given power in, (Luke 10:9 NIV), "I have given you authority to trample on snakes and scorpions and to overcome all the power of the enemy; nothing will harm you. However, do not rejoice that the spirits submit to you, but rejoice that your names are written in heaven." "At that time Jesus, full of joy through the Holy Spirit, said, "I praise you, Father, Lord of heaven and earth, because you have hidden these things from the wise and learned, and revealed them to little children. Yes, Father, for this is what you were pleased to do."

Be fearless, David found a reason to believe knowing he was fearfully and wonderfully made, due to God's handy works. When we know we don't have to be afraid the Lord God is faithful. That is why He says, "If you know the truth, the truth, will set you free." Do you know the truth? To know the truth our minds, have to be at peace. When we allow our minds to be at peace, we become strong and powerful to make more improvements and to empower the body of Christ. How should we empower others, one of the essential ways to empower others begins with understanding, love, and forgiveness. What does the Bible say about forgiveness? (Rom.8;1-4 NIV), "Therefore, there is now no condemnation for those who are in Christ Jesus, because through Christ Jesus the law of the Spirit who gives life has set you free from the law of sin and death. For what the law was powerless to do because it was weakened by the flesh, God did by sending his own Son in the likeness of sinful flesh to be a sin offering. And so, he condemned sin in the flesh, so that the righteous requirement of the law might be fully met in us, who do not live according to the flesh but according to the Spirit." The Lord is the Redeemer of our souls and Spirit.

Often, we find it so difficult to forgive others. Yet, to give it a command by the Lord God. "He says forgive them as I forgive you." forgiveness: What is forgiveness? "Forgiveness is a state that allows us to let go of our sins, and also, the ones who are trespasses against us." (Jer. 17:9-10 NIV), "The heart *is* deceitful above all *things and* desperately wicked; Who can know it? I, the Lord, search for the heart and test the mind. Even, to give every man according to his ways. According to the fruit of his doings." As Christians, we should not only find joy in happiness, but we must also convince ourselves to find joy in the struggles as well. Forgiveness is love, and it's the power that sets us free mentally, psychologically, and physically. Sadness is abnormal, which no one must experience it. How do you value sadness and happiness? So, allow yourself to rejoice for every moment.

Chapter #4

THE ARTS OF CREATIVITY

The cosmos reveals God's creativity. As you can see, creativity is art that is infinite art. E. g, "Davis was extremely skillful, due to his gifts and talents; King Saul found great pleasure in his skills. Not only David but also Prophet Daniel. He found favor from the King. "Daniel and his compatriots proved to be the wisest of all the trainees, and, at the end of their training, they entered the service of King Nebuchadnezzar. Daniel's first sign of faithfulness to God was when he and his three friends rejected the rich food and wine from the king's table, because they deemed it a defilement, and became vegetarians. As their health improved, they were permitted to continue with their chosen diet. In their education, the four men from Judah became knowledgeable in all Babylonian matters, and Daniel was given by God the ability to understand dreams and visions of all kinds." Creativity is a great source for every species, and we can do different things in our spot gradually and drastically, for we all are unique. Parents teach them to be confident and powerful. Children are born to become great through practical therapeutic. One of the easiest things to learn in life is through mistakes and everyone makes mistakes somehow. The one who never makes mistakes takes the risk. He/she is still naïve. It is best to go into life with someone more mature than fragile. "The world is but a canvas to the imagination." (Henry David Thoreau). We as God's children are His workmanship, created in Christ by Him in His image. It says in (Gen. 1:1NIV), "In the beginning, God created the heavens and the earth."

The universe indeed reveals God's handy works. When we look at the earth, the heaven, the moon, the stars, the sun, the sea, and the biomes in which we live. Creativity plays a magnificent role in the universe, and not only that but also in people's hearts. E.g, "In the beginning God created the heavens and the earth. "God loves the universe, that is why, when He looks at the universe, "He says let there be light." (Gen.1:1-5 NIV), "God said, "Let there be light," and there was light. God saw that the light was good, and he separated the light from the darkness. God called the light "day," and the darkness he called "night. "And there was evening, and there was morning the first day." As believers we should never conform to the pattern of this world. We should have desire to renew our minds daily to fucus on things we want to create. "As a man thinks in his heart so is he." No one has the power to devalue you; if you have confidence to know that you are gifted and talented.

According to, (Rom. 4:17 NIV), "As it is written: "I have made you a father of many nations." He is our father in the sight of God, in whom he believed the God who gives life to the dead and calls into being not." Creativity is simply thinking about the things that you want to create and display. The success of life folds in salvation through faith. And the Lord God has given us a measure of faith to excel at a higher detention through faith to fulfill our purpose. Abraham's purpose was to become a father of many nations. Yet he did not have any children when the Lord called him. However, the Lord God had to Calle upon those things prior to the things he will have to become. This is so profound! How do you perceive hope and faith? Don't give up on your children. For there is hope for them and know that every child is different and unique.

There is Hope for Every Circumstance

Success is mostly about preparation and the willingness to strive despite criticism and feelings. Be a role model for your child/ children don't lose hope. I am not saying that as a mechanism to encourage you. I am saying that as a fact. It is not about what the doctor said about your child/children. The reality is what you say or see and what you are willing to do to change the circumstances. One of my sons, the doctor, said he was artistic. I said no he is not. I reject the claim over my son's life. My son frequently has (an A+ or B+ but rarely has C. He graduated last May 24th in High school. He is the author of many books. Check out Jordan Narh-Martey's books on (Exlibrix.com. Besides He is involved in a new program. It says in (Prov.16:1 NIV), "To humans belong the plans of the heart, but from the Lord comes the proper answer of the tongue." Furthermore, It says in (Prov. 16:9 NIV), "In their hearts, humans plan their course, but the Lord establishes their steps." Your children have everything with them to excel at a greater level. If you want to become a role model in their lives. The skills they need to be successful in their career have been granted, in their gifts and talents. You need to ensure you position them in the right place because some people cannot manage the Golden Rule principles fairly.

According to (Exod. 35:23), "He has filled them with the skill to do all kinds of work as engravers, designers, embroiderers in blue, purple, and scarlet yarn and fine linen, and weavers all of them skilled workers and designers." Jesus said, "If you believe you will do greater work; then Him in the city." The challenges that you are going through are simply a process. You are more powerful than how people see you. We should always remember that we have been created in God's image, and we are God's inmost being. How do you value yourself? One of the easiest ways to become the finest person God intends for you to be. Is to love, believe in yourself, and be honest to yourself and others. You are worthy of all. We have everything within us to become whatever or to obtain whatever we want. Life consists of more things than money, gold, diamonds, and wealth. In special ways we have spiritual growth. Joy, love, peace, and happiness. Happiness will fade away, yet joy will remain the same. The way you love yourself, and to be loved and have confidence in yourself says it all. We must find a reason to be the "change we want to see take place." There is no need to be frustrated, you simply need to find what you have and be willing to utilize it for your benefit.

Every parent has the right to love, to support, and to protect their family. For, "No child shall live behind." Don't give up on your child/children. How do you value love and belief? "Love liberates," Jesus is of love through His love He came to set us free. Love is an act. If you find love for yourself and your child/ children, you will find a reason to improve yourself and impact others. The reality is not about how people view you. It all depends on how you view yourself in terms of positivity.

- Be confident
- Be stress-free
- Be faithful
- Be decisive
- Be committed
- Be hopeful
- Be willing

Chapter #5

FEARFULNESS OF LIFE

Parents represent the source that our children can draw from to build their future. Be decisive for the Lord God has not given us the spirit of fear. Life is not fair. Yet life is beautiful and meaningful. They are not alone, and they have everything they need to fulfill their destiny. Teach them to be confident and remind them that life is risky. They must face it with boldness. (Matt.11:12 NIV), "From the days of John the Baptist until now the kingdom of heaven suffered violence, and the violent take it by force." One of the most significant reasons that make life so beautiful and meaningful is the fact you exist in it created for a unique purpose. And being alive you have the power to change it to the way you want it to be. Remember if you want to see something change you must be the first to make that change.

Many people have been sick with "anxiety" and it is the # one killing people according to researchers. You have been created in God's image you have the power and dominion to decree and declare things. According to (Job. 22:28 NIV), "You will also declare a thing. And it will be established for you. So, light will shine on your ways." As it is written, I have made thee a father of many nations,) before him whom he believed, even God, who quickened the dead, and calleth those things which be not as though they were." Your child/children don't have to be under anxiety or depression for the rest of their lives. Be assertive, despite what David has been in the wilderness he found a reason to believe he is fearfully and wonderfully made.

E.g. The prodigal son thinks of himself if returns to his father things will change. According to "Luke 15:11-32 NIV), "A father had two sons. The younger son asked his father to give him the inheritance the father had promised him. Then, he went up to another country and spoiled all the money. Soon after, he found himself in poverty. He said to himself if he went back to his and asked him for forgiveness or asked him to work for things would be okay then to stay in that sad condition. As he made up his mind positively to go back to his father things changed for him amazingly. If you must change something in the life of your child/children at a greater level what will that be? For anxiety kills. One of the things that causes more anxiety is divorce. And it causes them to be unable to perform and "develop." And we all have a mission to fulfill.

Anxiety Is Sever:

From a spiritual standpoint, we should not be afraid of how we feel or see. "God not given us the spirit of fear." Yet power, love, self-discipline." Fear not. Allow God to manage your emotions rationally. The Lord God says, "He will never leave us or forsake us." So, learn to trust Him, all the way. Above all there is hope you may lose your spouse, or one of your loved ones. One thing that we must remember that "true love never dies." and besides, "people born to live and to die." Anyways God promises us He loves us unconditionally, and "He will always be with us." The reality is each day is a blessing; just to be alive. Regardless of what you have lost, believe that you can recapture everything in a blink. For any good thing can take place when you least expect it. Why don't you find a reason to be hopeful?

Cause and effect never lose it powers. However, we can count on God for He is the healer and the problem solver. There are things that have been taking place in our lives from DNA, in which we early perceive. E.g., when someone hits himself against something. Due to that problem something takes place by causes effect due to that issue. There are so many people that have suffered from all sorts of chronic disorders explicitly. We simply need to bring them to the Lord. To solve them; as the problem solver. And decide to love and to be loved even more, so that love will grow in every dry place. It says in (1 Cor. 13:7 NIV), "Love always protects, trusts, hopes, and perseveres.

As you may know. During the covid 19 nineteen; so many people have lost their loved ones. And besides that, everything has changed after the pandemic, and even now things have still not recovered. All that causes lots of problems for people. Yet we must find a reason to rise and shine for life to continue. The Lord says in, (1 Pet. 5:7 NIV), "Cast all your anxiety on Him because He cares for you." Despite the odds, we have to convince ourselves to know that whatever, life throws at us God cares for us and He is able to deliver us. That is why He says, "Fear not, for I am with you; be not dismayed, for I Am with you." Feel free to bring your problems at God's feet; for He cares for you. We should never forget all the things that the Lord God took for on Calvary. (Isa. 53:5 NIV), "He was wounded for our transgressions, bruised for our iniquities; and chastisement for our peace *was* upon Him, and by His stripes we are healed." Believe and know that whatever you have been lost God is able to re-embus them to you at a greater level. "Job is a witness of God's faithfulness. He lost all he had including his family." (Job.1:13-22 NIV), "Job's sons and daughters were having a feast in the home of his oldest son, when someone rushed up to Job and said, "While your servants were plowing with your oxen, and your donkeys were nearby eating grass, a gang of Sabeans attacked and stole the oxen and donkeys! Your other servants were killed, and I am the only one who escaped to tell you." E.g. Financial issues, social issues, loved one's issues, and so forth. I firmly believe that anxiety and depression can affect people from many perspectives. Yet we should always trust God; for He never fails.

Change is a fact of life, yet the Lord God never changes for He cares for us. So, there to be freedom despite the challenges of life. (Rom.8:38-39 NIV). "I am convinced that neither death nor life, neither angels nor demons, neither the present nor the future, nor any powers, neither height nor depth nor anything else in all creation, will be able to separate us from the love of God that is in Christ Jesus our Lord." So, above all the emotions, we are not alone, and besides we are loved by God! (Ps. 30:5 NIV), "This anger endures but a moment; in his favor is life: weeping may endure for a night, but joy cometh in the morning." Let us arise for joy is coming in the morning! May Jehovah Jireh grant you everything that you have lost. Just like He did for, "Abraham."

Force Yourself to see good in every challenge. Every child needs a variety of things to grow strong. Joseph had to face betrayal by his brothers to reach his destiny. (Gen. 50:20 NIV), "You intended to harm me, but God intended it for good to accomplish what is now being done, saving many lives." Perhaps he had to face challenges so that he could learn what forgiveness truly is. Sometimes our children must face hardship to become the person God intends for them. Joseph forgave his brothers after all they did to him. Forgiveness is one of the most significant elements that can change many things in people's lives.

One of the easiest ways to be stress-free is to learn to let go and allow God to manage the impossibility. For He is a great expert of all. When you know your problem is solvable and there is no need to be hangry. The moment you allow panic to come into your heart you lose power. E.g. "Peter got down out of the boat, walked on the water, and came toward Jesus. Yet, when he saw the wind, he was afraid and, beginning to sink, cried out, "Lord, save me!" Immediately Jesus reached out his hand and caught him. "You of little faith," He said, "why did you doubt?" As God's children, we must convince every circumstance to know that we are in overcomer. Because Jesus is with us. (Ps. 46:10 NIV), "Be still, and know that I am God: I will be exalted among the heathen, I will be exalted in the earth." Allow yourself to be at peace for the Lord God is on your side.

Anxious. According to, (Phi. 4:6-7 NIV), "Do not be anxious about anything, but in every situation, by prayer and petition, with thanksgiving, present your requests to God. And the peace of God, which transcends all understanding, will guard your hearts and your minds in Christ Jesus." Jesus told us in this life we will encounter lots of problems yet take heart for we already overcome them. "As a man thinks in his heart so is he." You have the power to control every struggle. As much as life is so beautiful, life also carries many tests. E.g. "King Solomon's life was not perfect. Yet he was not trying to feel guilty about his mistakes. Vanity of vanities, says the Preacher, vanity of vanities! All is vanity." Allow your pass behind you, fix your eye upon God. I have fought the good fight, I have finished the race, I have kept the faith. Now there is in store for me the crown of righteousness, which the Lord, the righteous Judge, will award to me on that day and not only to me but also to all who have longed for his appearance. Anxiety is not forever, there are ways you can bypass it positively. Life is not about winning, joy, love, peace. There is a time for every purpose under heaven. The more we perceive that the easier it will be to manage anxiety. Being honest with our children is wonderful. Therefore, they will know how to manage hardship, and it should be natural to go through some tough moments to discover your purpose.

Chapter #6

CHANGE IT NOT SIMPLY OCCURS BECAUSE YOU WISH

Change mostly takes place by a cause and willingness to remain in the process. As parents, as much as we want the best for our children, we must personal initiative for the outcome we intend to achieve. God in His infinite wisdom has created us in His image. His characteristics, His personality that's what we have. "Very truly I tell you, whoever believes in me will do the works I have been doing, and they will do even "greater" things than these because I am going to the Father. And I will do whatever you "ask" in my name, so that the Father may be glorified in the Son. You may ask me for anything in my name, and I will do it." Every child has some ups and downs as they grow up. It is up to us parents to still value them continue to love them stand with them to build a better future for them. Setbacks and failures cannot define your children or stop them from becoming what God sets out for them as you take responsibility to secure a brighter. No one can establish wealth or dreams on the things that you are not "valued." If you want your children to become successful in life, find a reason to love them despite their lack-ness. Obviously, one of the things that causes children to misbehave is "divorce" which leads to depression, low self-esteem, and dysfunction. How do you view your children in terms of value behavior?

Value for our children should come primarily from us. If you devalue them, it will be difficult for them to embrace themselves as they should. Every child is smart in different ways. That is why it is vital you love and value every one of your children. Then God said, "Let us make mankind in our image, in our likeness, so that they may rule over the fish in the sea and the birds in the sky, over the livestock and all the wild animals, and over all the creatures that move along the ground. Jesus said we are created in His image. How do think Jesus looks? So, presenting yourself in God's image on earth is essential. No one has ever seen Jesus, yet the cosmos reveals His handsomeness. When you present yourself in God's image you position yourself to increase at a greater level. Because we already have the confidence to overcome, improve, and empower our surroundings. According to (Peo. 27:7 NIV), "As a man thinks in his heart so is he." You can do all things if you simply believe. May you find a reason to believe again for we serve a God who is truly "Self-sufficient." (Cor. 5 NIV), "Not that we are competent in ourselves to claim anything for ourselves, but our competence comes from God." For He values us. Often, people misjudge us yet with confidence all is well for we know God loves and values us.

Wisdom and knowledge are reinsured in the time of low self-esteem not only that but also in the time of despair. Confidence despite what you have or going through sets a boundary if you are willing to maintain it. One of the easiest ways to set "boundaries" is to emulate good examples from God's throne room. For solely the truth we set ourselves free. "Every good thing begins with leadership and ends with leadership." "Everything thing falls on self-discipline. Self-discipline is the center of all dreams. Self-discipline allows us to face the risk, the fear, and the challenges to overcome whatever the circumstances are. You simply need faith to act for God already approved of all. During the process of becoming the person that God intends you to be. You may encounter lots of challenges. You need to have confidence in knowing that all is a part of the process of becoming a "problem" solver. What you perceive of yourself sets it all despite people's criticism for you know self-discipline is you. When it comes to self-discipline Jesus is one of the primary examples. Some children usually get fooled by taking treats from strangers. According to (Matt. 4:1-11 NIV), "**Then** Jesus was led up by the Spirit into the wilderness to be tempted by the devil. And when He had fasted forty days and forty nights, afterward He was hungry. Now when the tempter came to Him, he said, "If You are the Son of God, command that these stones become bread." Yet Jesus answered and said, "It is written, 'Man shall not live by bread alone, but by every word that proceeds from the mouth of God." Then the devil took Him up into the holy city, set Him on the pinnacle of the temple, and said to Him, "If You are the Son of God, throw Yourself down. For it is written: 'He shall give His angels charge over You,' and. In *their* hands, they shall bear you up. Lest you dash your foot against a stone." Despite the enemy's scheme, Jesus was able to use self-discipline to say no by utilizing God's words. (Pro. 22 NIV), "Train up a child in the way he should go; even when he is old, he will not depart from it." So, Jesus proves it a such a profound way. If you want your child/children to follow your foot points; as a great example what would that be? No one can make a change if he doesn't have the proper understanding of what the needs are. Getting to know your children and being responsible for structuring them is essential. What do you change for your children's future?

Chapter #7

CONFIDENCE

Confidence is the gear of our being to overcome every obstacle positively. Challenges often boost our confidence. Positivity gives us the courage we need when we face challenges that we don't focus on the problem only, yet we can see victory at the same time. When you look in the mirror what do you see besides what people say? Whatever you see in terms of confidence, ensure that you want the same thing for your children if you want them to overcome in their lives. "God has not given us the spirit of fear." Apostle Paul was on the verge of distress God told him my grace is sufficient for you. Even in times of struggle, we must find the courage to know we have all it takes to do whatever God intends us to be. Hold on firm to your confidence for you are not alone.

May the Lord grant you the strength that you need to overcome every struggle as you await upon the Lord. "They that wait upon the Lord shall renew their strength; they shall mount up with wings as eagles; they shall run, and not be weary; and they shall walk, and not faint." Despite the storm, you can overcome you need to simply position yourself at the right passion that brings pleasure to God's will. Obedience and courage give us the substance that will navigate our dreams. The more you embrace your goals, the better quality and quantity you will be able to produce. (Jer.29:11 NIV), "I know the plans I have for you," declares the Lord, "plans to prosper you and not to harm you, plans to give you hope and a future." It is imperative you have different types of mechanisms to nourish your goals and dreams to keep them from the right perspective. Remember there will be ups and downs time that will not be in your favor.

Persistence is one of the ultimate keys that will keep you focused on your destiny. You must have a reason to undertake your destiny seriously. "A good person leaves an inheritance for their children's children, but a sinner's wealth is stored up for the righteous." (Pro. 13:15 KJV). It is not enough to say you love your children without leaving them anything that's worthwhile. It is worth everything to leave them something as parents for them to begin to build their future for a better tomorrow. Your children need your love and support to have a brighter future for tomorrow. Plans fail for lack of counsel, but with many advisers, they succeed. Let us look at the story; there were some men and women who had impacted the world and left such a tremendous legacy to inspire others to take the leap of faith. Such as; Baker Eddy, Elizabeth Blackwell, and Susan B Antony. King David, King Solomon, and Abraham. Nothing is too difficult for Him. Intuition is to trust God beyond what you can see for the best is yet to come. "You don't get in life what you want, you get what you believe" Believe for your children there is a time for everything.

Everything goes with time and Jesus utilizes the time to create the cosmos accordingly. (Col. 1:16;20 NIV), "Through Him were all things created, that are in heaven, and that are in earth, visible and invisible, whether they be thrones, or dominions, or principalities, or powers: all things were created by Him and for Him." And He is before all things, and by Him all things consist of. According to Chapter 3:1-7 NIV),

- Day 1: God created light and separated it from darkness.
- Day 2: God created the sky, separating the waters above from the waters below.
- Day 3: God created the land and the seas and created plants and trees.
- Day 4: God created the sun, moon, and stars.
- Day 5: God created the creatures that live in the sea and the birds that fly in the sky.

- Day 6: God created the animals that live on the land and humans.
- Day 7: God rested.

Every child matters, And "No child should be left behind. Do you ever give up on your children? Everything has a time and purpose under the heavens on earth. What have you done recently? Attitude and Time play a significant role in our purpose. If you must do one thing today to draw closer to your dream or your "loved ones" what will that be? "Plans fail for lack of counsel, but with many advisers, they succeed." According to Proverbs 18:21 "Death and life are in the power of your tongue, and those who love them will eat the fruit of them." Through the difficulties you are facing, they are not there to disrupt you, they represent the bridge that you need to bring you the best outcome. Begin to speak blessing over your life and your children. (Gal. 6:9 NIV), "Let us not become weary in doing good, for at the proper time we will reap a harvest if we do not give up." Your hope for you and your promise will not be curt up. is not going to cut off. There is hope for every circumstance as you remain in prayer.

Never Give Up and Never Given on Your Children

We shall never become "weary of doing good at the proper time we will reap a harvest if we do not give up." As parents, we should never become frustrated with our dreams or material stuff. All will come at the proper time, for there is time for everything. (Matt. 6: 33 NIV), "Seek first His kingdom and His righteousness, and all these things will be given to you as well. But you have the power to retrieve your passion. It was not too for Sarah and Abraham, and so are you. Indeed, after my experience, it is not too you simply need to act, adapt, and maintain. You can do all the things you put your mind to if you believe. Be the world model you want your children to become. Everything you want to change be first to make that change gradually or drastically. Every child matters and no child should left behind. Dare to say blessings to your children. Regardless of the doctor's report, refuse to believe by faith. (Rom 4:17 NIV), "As it is written, I have made thee a father of many nations,) before him whom he believed, even God, who quickened the dead, and calleth those things which be not as though they were." There is power in God's word, and everything is conceivable in name. Put your hope in God.

There is hope for every season despite the odds when you believe. Hope keeps us going in the storm knowing that tomorrow will be better than today. "May the God of hope fill you with all joy and peace as you trust in him, so that you may overflow with hope by the power of the Holy Spirit. Optimism plays a major role in times of adversity it gives us the courage to push through regardless of our feelings. I have fought a good fight, I have finished my course, I have kept the faith: (2 Tim. 4:7 NIV), "I have fought a good fight, I have finished my course, I have kept the faith…"

Every child matters and "No child should left behind." regardless of their circumstances. Jesus said, "Let the little children come to "Me," and do not hinder them, for the kingdom of heaven belongs to such as these." How do you perceive your children? Despite David's background, he believes he was fully and wonderfully made. Thus, "You are fearfully and wonderfully made by God the Creator who has made you in His images." (Ps. 139:14 KJV). Adam and Eve have revealed the beauty of God's works. They were beautiful, they also had the opportunity to be fruitful and multiplied the land due to God's power. Joseph was a slave yet he made his bus became wealthier than before in Egypt. You have a reason to be grateful. (Isa. 40:31 "Those who hope in the Lord will renew their strength." They will soar on wings like eagles; they will run and not grow weary; they will walk and not be faint." Pray is the answer to everything if believe in God trust Him and be hopeful if you want greater things to manifest in your children's lives. Besides everything you could ever imagine in life, in terms of materials stuff. Yet life is still beautiful and with life, there is hope and it allows you to rejoice the best is yet to come.

God said, "One of the things that He enjoys the most is to see His children walking in the light." God's desire for His children is to be fruitful and multiply. Although, God has made the provision for us. If you had one objective towards humanity what would that be? (Matt. 18:5 NIV), "Whoever welcomes one such child in my name welcomes Me." How do you perceive hospitality? In terms of the destitute, and the sick? We all should be concerned towards others; particularly the ones who are the house faith. We all can become a patriot for God's glory. "Jesus said, "Whosoever, receives one little child like this receive Me." The profound things we can do it tangible, intangible, natural, and supernatural. I love My name receives Me." To invest in God's kingdom is one of the most wonderful things ever. Particularly in the lives of children because they represent the future of the next generation to keep the mission going.

Make a Wish for Children's Future

To make a wish for your children is essential. Above success happiness and fans. Many things are much more valuable. Whatever you want for your children can become a reality if you choose to be active in it and be passive. Effective parents are often active and not passive. Every parent must take personal initiative for their loved ones and not depend on others. Parents' DNA plays a significant role in every child's life. E.g. "All things have been committed to "Me" by my Father. No one knows the Son except the Father, and no one knows the Father except the Son and those to whom the Son chooses to reveal Him." Parents should never confuse, "active and proactive," because each of them carries its features. If King Solomon knew his life was going to be the way it was, he would select his wives according to his statutes. (1 (Kings 11:3 NIV), teaches us that he had many wives including concubines.

"He had seven hundred wives of royal birth and three hundred concubines, and his wives led him astray." At the end of his life, all his riches and fans. He regrets, that he said "Vanity of vanities, says the Preacher. "Vanity of vanities! All is vanity." What does man gain by all the toil at which he toils under the sun? A generation goes, and a generation comes, but the earth remains forever." **If clouds are full of water, they pour rain on the earth. Whether a tree falls to the south or the north, in the place where it falls, there it will lie." Every child matters. So, make a wise wish for your children. Money is so wonderful, yet some things will not fade away. Be**

proactive so that you will build the legacy you tend to be for your children. Perhaps King Solomon wanted to impress the world with his asserts and knowledge. But he wasn't too proud of it. It is not about pleasing the world but rather to please God.

Self-confidence plays a significant role in people's lives. It is not based on quantity nor the quality of things we have or do to prove it. Self-confidence is to know who you are and to be able to manage things accurately and morally. We are living in a "modern-day" in which everything is changing. Yet to be the best model for your children is the best thing ever. For one can walk in your "footsteps" if he hasn't felt them. What example do you want your children to take from you for a better future? As much as we want our children to have it all in terms of self-confidence, the seed must be planted; to bring forth the harvest. May the Lord God grant us the faith that we need to overcome every obstacle to fulfill our purpose.

Chapter #8

THE POWER OF SAFETY

Per-researchers "safety is a requirement. "For safety is not a gadget, but a state of mind." – (Eleanor Everet). Safety should be everyone's priority when it comes to mankind. In Effective parents don't have to wait for accidents to apply for safety. It should be done primarily. Safety is command as well as love. (Ps. 4;8 NIV), "The name of the Lord is a fortitude tower; the righteous run to it and are safe." There is safety for you in God's hands. Parents provide safety for their children for safety matters. Also, we do not want to lose anyone, particularly the best employees or the customers; children represent relationships for every life matter. Regardless of how safety we apply accidents can occur, but safety is better than "sorry." So, there is fire safety which calls for extinguishers that can prevent fire; so, injury and loss can take place at any time. Mercifully some great companies can cover you with affordable insurance to protect yourself and your loved ones.

Most businesses have policies when it comes to safety and everyone in the household or the organization that can protect everyone and everything. Family is a source that represents family safety and business safety to make it appeal and increase.

The Power of Dream

Every good parent dreams of having a child. And believe that child will become a legend or will be a great leader of the world. What is your dream about your child? Everything is possible and we should never stop dreaming for it is through dreams the vision becomes a reality. According to data, a dream is a series of thoughts images, visions, hope, as well as aspiration. Perhaps your definition of a dream may be different compared to that one. Truly it does not matter, it simply depends on the steps you take to develop it. A dream is a new thing that is not yet to come, in the natural way. To give birth to any dream, there must be preparation. Why do you need vision? It allows you to inspire yourself, as well as others; to keep them going in the right direction. Proverbs 11:14 says "Where no counsel is, the people fall: but in the multitude of counselors there is safety." Counsellors are so vital because regardless of your expertise, a good adviser will help you to conceptualize at another level to soar higher. Such as inventions, how to expend, capital, or industrialization, schools, hospitals, highways, and suburbs.

Planning for a vision helps it to stay on track and conceive it. Although, the vision is for some certain period. The most beautiful thing to do is prepare for it so that when the time comes you will be ready. What is on your agenda for your children's vision? To give birth to a solid vision you must keep it a priority and be willing to face criticism. You must know what to do daily to keep it going. What friend should I counsel to help me? Where Should I go for research? Dreams need time to build properly. Also, there are different types of mechanisms to construct it. It requires wisdom and knowledge. Therefore, you need to prepare in advance; that helps you navigate quickly in many directions that you need to go without disruption. You must have a certain time in mind to display the vision because you don't want to waste too much time in the dream when you place a time frame in the goal that inspires you to remain focused. The reason you need to come out at that time. Also, you need to know what to do with most of the success or benefit that you earn.

The Right Approach

Every child needs the perfect approach to become successful in life. Jesus is a miracle God, He has made the provision, so it's not a big deal for the paradigm to change. Being wealthy is a wonderful thing, but the most profound thing is to be joyful, at peace, active, and in good health to be able to enjoy every season and every horizon in your life. Just like Adam and Eve. Life has a way of making us obsessed by becoming so obsessed and forgetting how beautiful nature has been. Adam and his wife are the primary examples when it comes to enjoying nature. (Deut. 8:18) teaches us the Lord blessed Adam and his wife. "You shall [earnestly] remember the Lord your God, for it is He Who gives you the power to get wealth, that He may establish His covenant which He swore to your fathers, as it is this day." Therefore, God has given us access to the blessing. Now you must speak to your heart to bring it into reality. Job encourages us to call on "those things which are not as though they were. When was the last time you spoke blessings to your loved ones? It is essential to be the dower of the word. When was the last time you realest blessings and deliverance on your children? If you speak blessings and deliverance over your children, it will come to pass regardless of their circumstances. Eg., Joseph's dreams came to reality despite the odds that he went through. If your children are in captivity or any type of chaos may the Lord God grant you victory in Jesus' name. May your children get back into God's purpose for their lives.

Make a Wish for Children's Future

To make a wish for your children is essential. Above success happiness and fans. Many things are much more valuable. Whatever you want for your children can become a reality if you choose to be active in it and be passive. Effective parents are often active and not passive. Every parent must take personal initiative for their loved ones and not depend on others. Parents' DNA plays a significant role in every child's life. E.g. "All things have been committed to "Me" by my Father. No one knows the Son except the Father, and no one knows the Father except the Son and those to whom the Son chooses to reveal Him." Parents should never confuse, "active and proactive," because each of them carries its features. If King Solomon knew his life was going to be the way it was, he would select his wives according to his statutes. (1 (Kings 11:3 NIV), teaches us that he had many wives including concubines.

"He had seven hundred wives of royal birth and three hundred concubines, and his wives led him astray." At the end of his life, all his riches and fans. He regrets, that he said "Vanity of vanities, says the Preacher. "Vanity of vanities! All is vanity." What does man gain by all the toil at which he toils under the sun? A generation goes, and a generation comes, but the earth remains forever." **"If clouds are full of water, they pour rain on the earth. Whether a tree falls to the south or the north, in the place where it falls, there it will lie." Every child matters. So, make a wise wish for your children. Money is so wonderful, yet some things will not fade away. Be proactive so that you will build the legacy you tend to be for your children. Perhaps King Solomon wanted to impress the world with his asserts and knowledge. But he wasn't too proud of it. It is not about pleasing the world but rather to please God.**

Self-confidence plays a significant role in people's lives. It is not based on quantity nor the quality of things we have or do to prove it. Self-confidence is to know who you are and to be able to manage things accurately and morally. We are living in a "modern-day" in which everything is changing. Yet to be the best model for your children is the best thing ever. For one can walk in your "footsteps" if he hasn't felt them. What example do you want your children to take from you for a better future? As much as we want our children to have it all in terms of self-confidence, the seed must be planted; to bring forth the harvest. May the Lord God grant us the faith that we need to overcome every obstacle to fulfill our purpose.

Every Child Is Different

Every child is different than another and this is the beauty of every species. Despite the differences, they all have different gifts and are "unique." Every gift is crucial in the world. E.g., We as a body as much as the legs and the arms are different no one can say they aren't a part of each other. (1 Cor. 12:20-22 NIV), "As it is, there are many parts, but one body. The eye cannot say to the hand, "I don't need you!" And the head cannot say to the feet, "I don't need you!" On the contrary, those parts of the body that seem to be weaker are indispensable. Often, the child who seems so different is the most charming child among the rest. It doesn't matter how different your child is valuable in God's eye. E.g., Rachel and are sisters. Yet they describe Rachelle as the prettiest one. Yet the father by the name of Laban still did not want Rachel merry with Jacob first. He made a strategy for Leyah to marry Essau first.

Every parent has a responsibility towards their children, and every need must be met for them to fulfill their destiny. Every child's needs are different than the other. However, every parent must know what he/her needs is/are. And strives to achieve them. Every parent has to ask themselves who I am. And that will follow their responsibility as a mother or a father. Whatever your responsibilities are, ensure that you fulfill them. How well do you know your children? What do they want to become? It should be every parent's responsibility to stand on behalf of their children's future. Some of them you cannot do much, yet we should never give up. Every season brings something different. What would you like to take place in your children's future? What support would you be willing to provide as a dad/mom? What's the dream of your children?

According to (Gen. 25:27-28 NIV), "The boys grew up, and Esau became a skillful hunter, a man of the open country, while Jacob was content to stay at home among the tents. Isaac, who had a taste for wild games, loved Esau, but Rebekah loved Jacob. As parents, we should never allow differences to stop us from performing the duty we owe to every child. Every child has different needs that need to be met by their parents. How do you manage the differences in your children's lives particularly if you have tweens? The difference is so profound that's what brings forth genuineness in them. Often it is best for every one of them. Let us find a reason to love, support, and celebrate each child despite their conditions and differences! So, they can obtain a brighter future. God's desire is for them to be fruitful and multiply. "Beloved, I wish above all things that you mayest prosper and be in health, even as thy soul prospered."

"E.g. "God's **promise: Esau**'s descendants grew into a powerful nation, affirming that God's plans are intricate, far-reaching, and endure across generations." Esau was a hunter, and Jacob was quiet often by his mom. Esau's hair was red, hue, and covered in hair. Jacob fools Esau for his birthright. After the betrayal, they break up and are separated into different places. After a long time, they reconciled. (Gen. 33: 4), "Esau ran to meet Jacob and embraced him; he threw his arms around his neck and kissed him. And they wept." As parents, we should always remember the power of love and forgiveness.

Perhaps your children are in captivity or an orphanage. What do you promise your child? I want you to know that your presence plays a significant role in your children's spiritual lives. Jacob's mom ensured that Jacob obtained the blessing. "Man proposes yet God disposes Jacob encountered lots of problems in his life. "No Child Should Left Behind." Don't give up on your children!

How do you "value" your children? Children have been defined as genuine and a gift from above. Value plays a magnificent role in every child's life. The body of Christ is considered as the lilies, the apples. And the offspring in God's eye. The way you value your child will inspire you to invest in their future so that the future will be bright. Most people enjoy fruits. However, the fruit does not just happen to be in the tree. It requires a process, and the process demands to be maintained daily with the proper nutrients to nurture and bring forth good crops. You may not appreciate your children because they do not like other children you know. But it is not too late to bring forth whatever they might lose in their past. What is your duty to your child/children? What are your promises to them? Promise is one of the most important elements that always inspires people to do the impossible. It comes with will, responsibility, and commitment. "Train your children off on the way they should go, and even when they are old, they will not turn from it." Teach them to be dependable, reliable, confident, and positive. As much as Jacob and Essau's gift was different. Yet that did not define them as becoming what God intended for them to be. "Every child is matter and none of them shall left behind." For they are the future of the next generation.

Overall, joy will come. Dare to believe that these two shall pass away. For every problem is in an open bridge for a new horizon. Believe in your children and know that "No child shall left behind." And never give up on your children. For they represent the future of the next generation. Dare to leave an inheritance for them so they can utilize it as a bridge to build their future. Children are divine from the "Father of light." (Matt.18:3 NIV), "Truly I tell you, unless you change and become like little children, you will never enter the kingdom of heaven." "There can be no keener revelation of a society's soul than the way in which it treats its children." (Nelson Mandela). Let us find a reason to love, protect, guide, and take the responsibility that every parent owes to their beloved children. For, "No child shall left behind." For it is the parents' responsibility.

www.ingramcontent.com/pod-product-compliance
Lightning Source LLC
Chambersburg PA
CBHW051248120626
46547CB00014B/1851